A souvenir guide

Runnymede and Magna Carta

Surrey

National Trust

The Most Famous Meadow in the World

Runnymede in Surrey is an open green space by the side of the Thames, used extensively for leisure and recreation by local people. The serenity of the landscape is interrupted today by cars travelling to and from the M25 motorway and by planes taking off and landing at Heathrow airport. Despite the intrusions of modernity, however, this remains perhaps the most famous meadow in the world because of the events that took place here in June 1215: the sealing of Magna Carta.

Runnymede before Magna Carta

Runnymede's significance, however, has a far longer history, stretching back as far as the Neolithic period. Excavations in advance of the construction of the M25 revealed evidence of an extensive late Bronze Age settlement around the area of Runnymede Bridge. Among the objects recovered were a spearhead, polished stone axes, rings, buttons, amber beads, plenty of pottery and two pairs of tweezers. Prehistoric swords have also been retrieved from the Thames at this spot.

So it is likely that Runnymede's riverside location has long held symbolic importance, as well as being on one of the main communication and trading routes in and out of London. The choice of Runnymede as the site where Magna Carta was agreed in 1215 may also reflect its proximity to the royal castle at Windsor, first established in the 11th century.

The Angevin dynasty

The events of June 1215 cannot be understood without first appreciating the political background that led to King John agreeing to the demands of his barons. The significance of Magna Carta lay in the restrictions it imposed on the powers of the King.

The reign of Henry II from 1154 marked the beginning of the rule of the Angevin kings, the first of the Plantagenet dynasties. Plantagenets were to retain control of the English throne for more than three hundred years, until Richard III was defeated at Bosworth Field in 1485.

Henry II was succeeded by his sons, first Richard I in 1189, then his youngest son John after Richard's death in France in 1199. This Angevin dynasty derived its name from the French region of Anjou, reflecting the fact that their territorial control stretched from England down through France as far as the Pyrenees.

Bad King John

The Angevins had a reputation for cruelty and absolutism, and none more so than King John. Having to fight wars in France to defend his territories meant that John was continually seeking to raise money from his subjects through fines and other forms of taxation.

In addition, John surrounded himself with favoured advisers and allies, many of them French. To these confidants John would allot lands and castles, further antagonising the more established barons and their families. John's court became a byword for intrigue and paranoia. King John is remembered by posterity as a fundamentally 'bad' king. After John's death the chronicler Matthew Paris recorded that 'black as is Hell, John's presence there makes it blacker still'.

Left The riverside meadows of Runnymede

Above King John (1167–1216)

Far left A picnic by the Thames on August Bank Holiday 1939

The barons

The primary cause of the events of 1215 was the perception that John had been excessive in the demands he placed on his barons. Rumours of rebellion were rife.

Since the Norman Conquest of 1066 England had been under the control of a powerful aristocratic elite, who held their lands from the King in return for performing military service. The King was able to take advantage of their position of legal dependence to exact dues from them and take temporary possession of their lands in the event of an heir's minority (wardship).

The King raised money by imposing taxes on his subjects, in order to finance his military campaigns in France, Ireland, Wales and Scotland.

The rebellion grows

After negotiating a settlement with the Pope in May 1213, John declared England and Ireland to be papal fiefdoms. He prepared to invade France, in order to defend his territories. But many barons refused the order to support him.

John met disaffected barons from the north and midlands at Wallingford in November 1213, and pledged to uphold their liberties. But the promise was hollow. Many barons continued to refuse to serve the King or finance his wars.

The barons unite

By the end of 1213 there were strong reports that something needed to be done to restrain the King. While John was planning a military campaign in France, he left Peter des Roches, bishop of Winchester, to act as governor in England.

In July 1214 John suffered a significant blow when his ally, the Emperor Otto of Germany, was defeated at the Battle of Bouvines. Not only was his half-brother William Longespée captured, but at home yet more barons joined the ranks of the discontented. Increasingly, the talk was of how to compel John to recognise the limits that his forebears had observed in earlier coronation charters. The barons wanted to restore order, and to limit John's ability to raise money and go to war at will.

A significant meeting took place in Bury St Edmunds in the autumn of 1214. Here, a group of barons is said to have agreed to take up arms against the King, if he continued to abuse his position. A memorial near St Edmundsbury Cathedral marks the occasion.

Opposite Samuel Phelps as King John in Shakespeare's play *King John*, which does not mention Magna Carta

Left John suffered a major defeat at the Battle of Bouvines in July 1214

Opposite The barons rebel against the King. This colour postcard was produced for the 1907 Bury St Edmunds Magna Carta pageant

The road to Runnymede

The King was finally forced to agree to the terms of a settlement with his barons at Runnymede in June 1215. This agreement, which John tore up soon afterwards, is nevertheless considered one of the turning points of English history.

The early months of 1215 saw the barons gaining confidence in the demands they were making of their king. They demanded that John abolish the 'evil customs' that had grown up around him, as previous monarchs had done. (Henry I had issued a charter on his coronation in 1100 giving an assurance that he would govern in this way, although in truth he also failed to live up to these expectations.)

The barons met at Brackley in May 1215 and withdrew their support for the King. John responded by ordering the capture of several of the barons' castles.

On 17 May, the City of London pledged allegiance to the barons and their cause. This was a hugely significant development, given London's historic independence from the King and its importance to the economic and political life of the nation. John was compelled to negotiate a truce with his barons.

Why Runnymede?

The 'Charter of Liberties' was finally agreed between John and his barons on 15 June 1215. Detailed analysis of early drafts of the document demonstrates that changes were being made right up until the King's seal was applied, as both sides settled on a carefully negotiated form of words for each of the 63 chapters.

The Charter ended by declaring that it had been 'Given by our hand in the meadow that is called Runnymede, between Windsor and Staines'. Yet nobody knows with any certainty why Runnymede was chosen, or the precise spot where the agreement was finalised. There is no extant archaeology at Runnymede to link the present-day site of the meadows to the events of June 1215.

Between Windsor and Staines

One reason why Runnymede may have been selected is the fact that it sat midway between the King's base at Windsor and Staines, where the barons were based and which marked the edge of the City of London's jurisdiction. Other theories – that the document was sealed on the site now known as Magna Carta Island, for instance, or the idea that it may have been agreed at Ankerwycke Priory, on the other side of the river – remain the stuff of speculation and myth-making.

Left A romanticised late 18th-century vision of King John sealing Magna Carta; coloured engraving after Benjamin West

Right Runnymede from Cooper's Hill with a distant view of the round tower of Windsor Castle; painted by E.J. Niemann

The Great Charter

Magna Carta, as it came to be known, is now remembered as a milestone on the route to democracy and individual freedoms. Yet it is hard to see the Charter agreed in June 1215 as anything other than a fundamentally conservative document, seeking the restoration of traditional forms of governance. Magna Carta's later significance therefore exceeds its literal meaning.

The Charter agreed at Runnymede in 1215 consisted of 63 separate chapters, each rectifying an area where it was perceived that King John had overstepped the mark of what a king was entitled to do. Much of it was concerned with the day-to-day working of feudal relations. Several of the chapters related to the circumstances in which the crown could claim payments from its subjects, or the various fines and fees that lubricated the moving parts of medieval government. The concepts of freedom promulgated in the Charter were 'liberties' from excessive interference by the King. Chapter 30 ensured that royal officials were denied the ability to seize horses or carts for transport from free

Right A colour facsimile of Magna Carta published following the fire at Ashburnham House in Westminster in 1731, in which the original (now in the British Library) was badly damaged. The coats of arms belong to the barons who forced King John to agree to Magna Carta

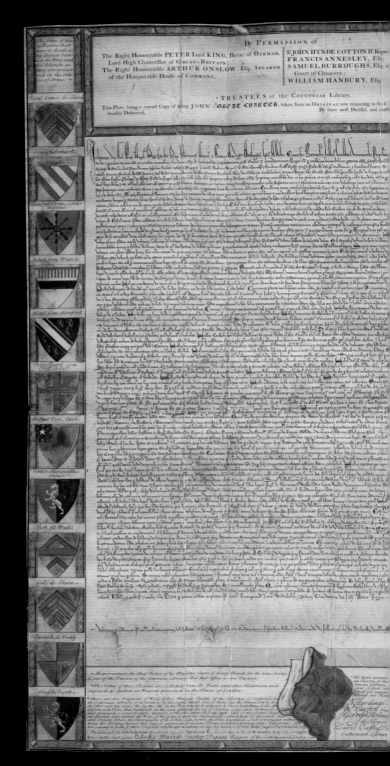

men without their consent, while chapter 52 restored lands and castles that had been arbitrarily seized by King John without the consent of the barons. To resolve future disagreements, a standing body of 25 barons was proposed, who would pass judgement on whether the King was acting lawfully. The chapters of the Charter that continue to speak to us, 800 years later, are those relating to justice and the law. Chapters 39 and 40 in particular have laid down principles – of the right to a fair trial, and the right against unlawful imprisonment (habeas corpus) – that still stand today.

Above A facsimile of the copy of Magna Carta formerly at Lacock Abbey in Wiltshire

The most significant chapters of Magna Carta

- To no one will we sell, to no one deny or delay right or justice (chapter 40)

- No free man shall be seized or imprisoned … except by the lawful judgement of his equals or by the law of the land (chapter 39)

- The English Church shall be free, and shall have its rights undiminished, and its liberties unimpaired (chapter 1)

- Earls and barons shall be fined only by their equals, and in proportion to the gravity of their offence (chapter 21)

- The City of London shall enjoy all its ancient liberties and free customs (chapter 13)

Iohannes rex genuit videlicet

The fall and rise of Magna Carta

In truth, the Charter of 1215 was a failure. Within months, it had been annulled, and the King was once more at war with his barons. But it was revived on the accession of Henry III, and its significance was to grow in the years that followed.

The Charter of June 1215 had only a short life. By September, following a tense summer of simmering conflict, the King announced that he rejected the terms of the Charter. Formal annulment by the Pope followed shortly afterwards, with the document declared as a demeaning, unjust and shameful imposition upon the monarch.

Civil war ensued, as the rebel barons sided with Prince Louis, son of the King of France, who arrived in London to claim the crown. The First Barons' War witnessed sieges at the important castles of Dover, Rochester and Windsor. John's reign ended not long afterwards, in ignominy. Attempting to cross the Wash, his ship is said to have sunk along with the crown jewels. Having contracted dysentery, he died at Newark in October 1216.

Magna Carta reissued

Following John's death, his nine-year-old son was crowned as Henry III with William Marshal as regent. Soon after, Magna Carta was reissued, on Marshal's advice, as the new king's coronation charter. It was issued again in November 1217 after the peace with Louis, but this time the clauses relating to forest law were extracted and put into their own document, the Charter of the Forest. Those remaining formed the larger document, and to differentiate it from the forest charter it started to be referred to as the Great Charter or Magna Carta.

The Charter of the Forest

Much in the original 1215 charter related to King John's extension of forest law across an ever-wider territory of land. Land under forest law was managed for the king's benefit in providing deer and other game, and punishments for falling foul of forest law were draconian. The Charter of the Forest of 1217 rolled back the extensions of royal forest lands under King Richard and King John. It also enshrined various liberties in relation to the use of forest lands for grazing pigs and other forest activities:

- Every free man shall have the right to collect wood and pasture his pigs in the forest as he wishes

- No one shall henceforth lose life or limb because of our venison

Left King John hunting in a royal forest; a 14th-century illuminated manuscript

Below The tomb of King John in Worcester Cathedral

The legacy of Magna Carta

Magna Carta's legacy lies in the symbolism it subsequently assumed in the decades and centuries that followed the events of 1215. The document came to stand for a set of principles – liberty, justice, freedom under the law – that went far beyond the intentions of its original authors. As the times changed, so did the significance and authority of the language of the Charter.

Magna Carta was reissued nearly a dozen times in Henry III's reign alone, generally at periods of crisis when the King needed to stabilise a volatile political situation. The Charter was last reissued in 1300 by Edward I, by which time its status as a bulwark of the English constitutional framework had been confirmed. Official readings of Magna Carta by state officials would continue to be heard on special occasions, such as the opening of Parliament. The manuscript collections of statutes used by lawyers commonly started with Magna Carta, and these were circulated widely with the advent of commercial printing.

Although there was less heed paid to Magna Carta in the Tudor era (Shakespeare famously did not refer to it at all in his play about King John), by the civil wars of the mid-17th century its legacy was being revived. Lawyers such as Sir Edward Coke, the Lord Chief Justice, wrote commentaries on its significance as a turning point in the development of ideas of personal liberty and its contemporary political relevance. Two hundred years later, the Chartists of the 19th century also made direct allusion

Opposite *Liberty suspended!* This cartoon of 1817 by George Cruikshank attacks Lord Eldon for threatening the British constitution by gagging the Press. The bound and gagged figure of Liberty hanging from the gibbet holds a scroll inscribed 'Magna Charta, Bill of Rights, Habeas Corpus'

Below The signing of the United States Declaration of Independence in 1776. The Declaration was strongly influenced by Magna Carta

to Magna Carta in their campaign for democratic freedoms.

Such mythologising of the original meaning of Magna Carta went far beyond England alone. In America, the ideas associated with Magna Carta had a strong influence on the Declaration of Independence and the Bill of Rights.

Magna Carta has continued to exert an influence on the development of thinking about rights and freedoms to the present day. The language of Magna Carta can be heard in the United Nations' Universal Declaration of Human Rights of 1948.

Left Rosedene Cottage in Worcestershire was built by the National Land Company as part of the Chartist Land Plan

A meadow in time

Runnymede retained its open character as meadowland in the centuries that followed the events of 1215. Until the Dissolution of the Monasteries in the 1530s the manor of Egham was in the possession of Chertsey Abbey, but thereafter it was held by the Crown.

From February to August the land was left for hay-growing. After the hay crop had been gathered, Old Lammas Day (12 August) marked the start of the grazing season. The meadow was grazed first by cattle and horses, and then by sheep from November to February.

So important was Runnymede as an open space that it was given special treatment in the Egham Enclosure Act of 1814. The Act decreed that the meadow should remain unfenced, at a time when enclosure acts elsewhere were carving up commons into separate plots.

Egham Races

The principal reason why Runnymede was spared enclosure was not its association with Magna Carta, but the fact that the meadows had become the site of an annual horse racing meeting. The Egham races began in 1734, and were revived in the late 18th and early 19th centuries.

Left The Egham race course in 1824

'That ever-to-be famous June morning'
Runnymede features in Jerome K. Jerome's comic novel, *Three Men in a Boat* (1889):

'The sun had got more powerful by the time we had finished breakfast, and the wind had dropped and it was as lovely a morning as one could desire. Little was in sight to remind us of the nineteenth century; and, as we looked out upon the river in the morning sunlight, we could almost fancy that the centuries between us and that ever-to-be famous June morning of 1215 had been drawn aside.'

King William IV attended one event, and gave a speech in which he reminded the crowds 'that it was here that our liberties were obtained and ever secured'.

The last official race meeting was held in 1884, by which time the crowds had become so rowdy that the police were no longer willing to provide security. The only physical evidence for the former race track today are gaps in the hedges at Runnymede.

Spoilt by gas works
By the early 20th century, the effects of industrialisation and urbanisation were being felt. One visitor writing in 1914 observed that: 'The river bank is spoiled by gas works, bungalows, and other excrescences for part of the way … if the public do not take heed they may soon awake to the fact that Runnymede has been covered with suburban housing.'

Above Langham Pond and the water meadows around it remained unenclosed throughout the 19th century

Left Egham races in 1880

The Saving of Runnymede

In the early 20th century, Runnymede was under threat. As an open green space near London, it was viewed as prime development land. The proposed sale of the land by the Government generated a public outcry, and led ultimately to its purchase by the Broughton family, who gifted it 'to the nation' by transferring it to the National Trust.

Opposite A view from Cooper's Hill over Runnymede in the late 19th century; painted by Robert Gallon

Below The view from Cooper's Hill over the Runnymede water meadows today

After the First World War, the coalition Government under David Lloyd George was looking for ways to reduce the public debt. By this time, the meadows had become a popular place of resort at weekends, for picnics and recreation. Lloyd George himself was reported to have said that the meadows would make a fine permanent fairground. He was clearly thinking of the value the land would realise were it to be sold.

In 1921 Helena Normanton spotted that 252 acres (102 hectares) of crown land in Egham, including the meadows at Runnymede, described merely as 'Lot 8', were being put up for sale. On hearing of the plan for Runnymede, she sprang into action, writing letters to *The Times* and others in protest.

Soon Normanton had gathered some notable supporters, including the Marquess of Lincolnshire, who raised the matter in the House of Lords, and the local vicar, Rev. Albert Cecil Tranter. The three of them founded the Magna Carta Society, to act as guardians for the site.

A furious row ensued. At a League of Nations' meeting, Tranter said he would 'throw into the Thames any auctioneer who should attempt to sell Runnymede'.

The public outcry at the sale was such that the Government was forced to back down. In August 1921 Sir Arthur Griffith Boscawen, Minister for Agriculture, announced that the 99 acres (40 hectares) of Runnymede meadows were to be withdrawn from the sale.

Guardian of Runnymede
Helena Normanton was a talented lawyer as well as a campaigner for women's rights. She became the first woman in England to practise as a barrister, having won a landmark legal fight that allowed her to use her maiden name in her professional practice.

Runnymede for the nation

Realising that the future of the meadows was far from secure, Normanton and her colleagues agreed that annual meetings should be held at Runnymede to keep up the public pressure. Each year, prominent public figures were invited to give speeches in honour of Magna Carta and the site where it was sealed.

Eventually a more permanent solution was found, following the intervention of the Broughton family, who lived near Runnymede at Englefield Green.

Urban's wife, Cara, was given the title Lady Fairhaven in May 1929. The title intended for her husband passed to her eldest son, who became the 1st Lord Fairhaven.

In memory of Urban, Lady Fairhaven and her sons purchased the meadows at Runnymede in December 1929 and passed them to the National Trust two years later. The meadows had at last been saved for the nation.

A wealthy supporter of good causes

Urban Broughton, an English-born civil engineer, made his fortune in America where he lived from 1887. Returning to England with his American wife and two sons in 1912, Urban became MP for Preston during the First World War. He and his wife used their wealth and influence to support good causes, and Urban was eventually nominated for a peerage. Before he could assume his title, however, Urban Broughton died, in January 1929.

Helena Normanton was overjoyed that Runnymede had been rescued from development. 'It is a repulsive thought,' she wrote, 'that our children's children might have had to seek the site whereon our country's liberties were obtained beneath a clustering covey of bungalows something like Peacehaven!'

Left The water meadows in 1931; painted by E.B. Waggett

Right Cara, Lady Fairhaven; painted by Oswald Birley

A memorial landscape

Following the permanent saving of Runnymede for the nation, the site has become a memorial landscape, alongside its continuing use for agriculture and recreation. As well as monuments to Magna Carta, Runnymede is now home to memorials to those who lost their lives serving in the air force, as well as to President Kennedy. In this way the abiding symbolic significance of Runnymede, as meaningful to its prehistoric settlers as to the protagonists of 1215, continues to resonate in the modern era.

In the 20th century, three of the country's most distinguished architects and designers were each commissioned to make new interventions at Runnymede. Through their

creations, Sir Edwin Lutyens, Sir Edward Maufe, and Sir Geoffrey Jellicoe all left their mark on the Runnymede landscape, turning it into a site of memorialisation and reflection.

The Lutyens memorials

In association with Lady Fairhaven's acquisition of Runnymede, the architect Sir Edwin Lutyens was commissioned to design a number of structures in memory of both Urban Broughton and Magna Carta.

At the Windsor end of the site, Lutyens placed two distinctive lodge buildings and beside them two plinths on either side of the road carrying monumental inscriptions. The plinths are of Portland stone and echo Lutyens's design of the Cenotaph in Whitehall.

At the opposite end, towards Egham, two smaller kiosks were placed in a similar arrangement, also with plinths.

The two lodge buildings are currently used by the National Trust as a café and offices. In September 1939 they became, briefly, the main national office for the Trust, when its London office was evacuated on the outbreak of war.

Above Lutyens also designed the memorial kiosks at the south end of the meadows; watercolour by Cyril Farey, 1930

Left Inscriptions on the plinths record the Fairhavens' bequest to the National Trust

Opposite The Fairhaven lodges were designed by the great architect Edwin Lutyens

The Commonwealth Air Forces Memorial

Just above the tree line of Cooper's Hill Woods is a striking memorial to over twenty thousand airmen and women who died in the Second World War but who have no known grave. The memorial was designed by Sir Edward Maufe, the principal architect for the Commonwealth War Graves Commission after the war, and unveiled in October 1953.

The siting of the Air Forces Memorial so near to Runnymede was not without significance. Dedicating the site at the official opening ceremony, the Queen referred to the historic link between Runnymede and ideas of freedom: 'For wherever and for as long as freedom flourishes on the earth, the men and women who possess it will thank them and will say that they did not die in vain.'

The American Bar Association Memorial

Sir Edward Maufe was also the architect of a striking monument that now occupies a location on the lower slopes of Cooper's Hill. The American Bar Association in 1957 commissioned the memorial, which is a classical Greek temple in Portland stone. Below its striking star-spangled dome sits a granite pillar carved in commemoration of Magna Carta, 'Symbol of Freedom Under Law'. The memorial and the land on which it stands are vested in the Magna Carta Trust.

The Kennedy Memorial

Another leading landscape architect of his day, Sir Geoffrey Jellicoe, designed a monument to President John F. Kennedy, which was unveiled by the Queen in 1965. The centrepiece is a seven-ton block of Portland stone, engraved with a passage from the President's inaugural address. The monument, based on Bunyan's *The Pilgrim's Progress*, is reached by means of a steep path made from irregular granite setts, 60,000 in total. The land on which it sits was given to the USA, and is therefore officially American soil.

The Jamestown Oak

Near the Magna Carta Memorial stands another reminder of the close links between England and America. An oak tree was planted here in December 1987 using soil from Jamestown, Virginia, the first permanent English settlement in the New World. The tree was planted to mark the bicentenary of the Constitution of the United States of America.

Far left The Magna Carta Memorial was commissioned by the American Bar Association

Left The steps up to the Kennedy Memorial are made of 60,000 granite setts

Top The Kennedy Memorial

Above The Queen greets Jacqueline Kennedy, her children and brother-in-law, Robert Kennedy, at the unveiling of the Kennedy Memorial in 1965

Runnymede Today

Flora and fauna

Runnymede consists of a diverse patchwork of habitats, which continue to evolve. The site is famed for its low-lying pasture and hay meadows, which include very herb-rich unimproved grassland. The slopes of Cooper's Hill Wood are dominated by ancient semi-natural broadleaved woodland. A series of spring-fed ponds, marginal swamp and reedbed habitats can also be found.

River

Runnymede is located in the middle reach of the Thames. The river defines the local area, and is now used mainly for leisure purposes such as pleasure boating, canoeing and angling. The Thames Path National Trail passes by Runnymede and is a popular walking route.

Because the Runnymede meadows are on the flood plain, they are frequently covered in water, when the Thames overtops its banks.

Above Langham Pond is an important wetland habitat for dragonflies and damselflies

Meadows

Many birds frequent the meadows, including Red Kite, Buzzard, Swallow and House Martin. Some birds stay to breed within the long grasses of the meadows including the Skylark.

The invertebrate life that can be found here includes Cinnabar Moth, Common Blue Butterfly, and lots of Azure Coenagrion puella damselflies.

The main grasses present within the meadows include false oat-grass and perennial rye-grass with frequent Yorkshire fog. Wild flowers include Creeping Buttercup, Common Sorrel, Tufted Vetch and Field Scabious, as well as rarer plants such as Marsh Stitchwort.

Woodland

Veteran oak trees can be found within Cooper's Hill Wood. These support a wide variety of wildlife including Nationally Notable species of invertebrates. The Soprano Pipistrelle and Brown Long-eared bats have been recorded here. Bird species present include the Song Thrush, Green Woodpecker and Stock Dove. Runnymede has also seen an increasing number of the non-native Ring-necked Parakeet.

Langham Pond Wetland

Langham Pond is one of the most important ponds in the country for nature conservation. It is particularly rich in dragonflies and damselflies, with 27 different species having been identified here so far. Common species include the Emperor Dragonfly and Banded Demoiselle along with Azure Blues. Rare water beetles can also be found.

Plants found here include Yellow Flag, Meadow Sweet, Flowering Rush and the particularly rare Greater Water Parsnip, Frogbit and Tubular Water-dropwort.

Birds that frequent the wetland area include Grey Heron, White Throat, Mandarin, Moorhen, Coot, Lapwing, Swan, Pied Wagtail and Reed Warbler, Cuckoo and Reed Bunting.

Left Red kites are an increasingly common sight soaring over the meadows of Runnymede

Left below An Emperor dragonfly

Below Field Scabious

Ankerwycke

On the other side of the river to Runnymede is another property owned and cared for by the National Trust, the Ankerwycke estate. Ankerwycke is home to by far the oldest historic features in the local landscape, which would have witnessed the sealing of Magna Carta.

Ankerwycke was a farmed estate, which formerly featured a fine family house, pleasure gardens, and several other villas. The main house at Ankerwycke has now been demolished, but the garden paths survive. One 19th-century writer recorded that the gardens here were 'filled with flowers, fragrant and of every hue', and also boasted a kitchen garden and extensive greenhouses.

The National Trust acquired the estate in 1998, principally to secure the views from the Runnymede meadows. Ankerwycke is 148 acres (60 hectares) of parkland currently grazed under licence.

Nestling in the heart of the Ankerwycke woods are the remains of a Benedictine priory, founded in the reign of Henry II by Sir Gilbert Mountfitchet and his son, Sir Richard Mountfitchet. The priory was dedicated to Mary Magdalene. Sir Richard's son, also Richard, was one of the 25 barons who brought John to the negotiating table in June 1215.

Nearby stands the Ankerwycke Yew. This 2,500-year-old tree would already have been considered ancient by the time of the events of 1215. Henry VIII is said to have courted Anne Boleyn here.

Magna Carta Island, on the north bank of the river, also formed part of the Ankerwycke estate in the 19th century. In 1834 a house was built on the island by George Simon Harcourt, and an erroneous claim was made for this as the site where Magna Carta was sealed.

Enjoying the riverside
Runnymede Pleasure Gardens, which neighbours Runnymede to the east, sits on the Thames Path. The gardens comprise a 16-acre (6-hectare) amenity park owned and managed by Runnymede Borough Council, containing a café, playground, lido, car-park and playing field. In keeping with the way Runnymede came to be used in the early 20th century, the pleasure gardens are popular with families and others for recreation and the chance to enjoy the riverside.

Above The Ankerwycke Yew is over 2,500 years old

Opposite The hollowed-out centre of the Ankerwycke Yew makes a great place to play

Left The ruins of St Mary's Priory

Celebrating Magna Carta over 800 years

The anniversary of the sealing of Magna Carta has been marked in different ways in the past. In the 20th century, as the threats to the site grew ever greater, Runnymede was regularly used for annual gatherings and services.

Printed in gold
On the occasion of its 600th anniversary, a special edition of the Charter was produced by John Whittaker, in which the letters were printed in gold leaf. A copy is to be found in the library of Anglesey Abbey, the home of Urban Broughton's eldest son, the 1st Lord Fairhaven.

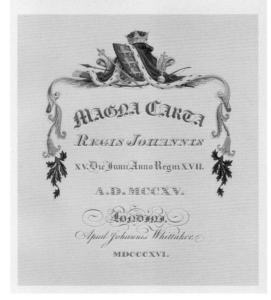

Such gatherings were mirrored by similar meetings in other towns with close associations with Magna Carta. At the height of the initial controversy over the sale of Runnymede, Helena Normanton visited Bury St Edmunds, to learn how they organised the pageants that took place there.

There had been an idea to hold a pageant on Runnymede in 1915 to commemorate the 700th anniversary, but the First World War disrupted these plans.

GWEN LALLY

Far left The vicar of Staines, the Rev. J.R. James, learning to ride an elephant for the 1934 Magna Carta Pageant

Left Theatrical impresario Gwen Lally, who directed the 1934 Magna Carta Pageant

The 1934 pageant was orchestrated by theatrical impresario Gwen Lally, who also directed pageants on a similarly epic scale at Warwick Castle and Langley Park, Slough. Lally described her shows as being like a 'silent super-film, but filled in with appropriate battle cries, songs and acclamations'.

The pageant of 1934

In 1934 the meadows played host to an extraordinary pageant in commemoration of Magna Carta. The pageant comprised an extravagant sequence of scenes from English history, involving more than 5,000 performers (many drawn from the local area) as well as leading actors of the day such as Sybil Thorndike and Scott Sunderland.

Magna Carta 800

On 15 June 2015 Runnymede plays host to the world as we commemorate the 800th anniversary of the sealing of Magna Carta. The day will be an exciting celebration of the Foundation of Liberty through Magna Carta, animated through music, debate, drama, spoken word and social media. It looks to the future as much as to the past. Complementary events are also taking place in the Charter Towns and in the libraries that hold copies of Magna Carta.

The Foundation of Liberty through Magna Carta celebrates the contribution of Magna Carta in the spread of liberty, democracy, human rights and the rule of law throughout the world. The event is intended to:

- Demonstrate the relevance of Magna Carta, locally, nationally and internationally.

- Reaffirm the principles of rule of law, fair justice, equality and safety from the abuse of governmental or judicial power.

- Promote the vital importance of individual rights and acknowledge the role of Parliament in promoting these rights.

- Acknowledge Magna Carta's impact on constitutional and democratic development since 1215.

Left **Hew Locke at Runnymede**

In the morning Runnymede is the setting for an international state occasion. As part of the morning activities a major new art installation will be unveiled. This is the work of Hew Locke, one of Britain's most outstanding contemporary artists, and has been made possible by the kind support of Surrey County Council. In the afternoon the mood becomes more festive, as the historic meadows host Parliament's national LiberTeas. LiberTeas is a chance to celebrate and debate your rights, and is part of Parliament's special anniversary programme for 2015 (www.parliament.uk/2015).

Entry will only be possible with a ticket. For more information on how to get your free ticket, please visit the National Trust Runnymede website at www.nationaltrust.org.uk/runnymede.

A lasting legacy

Our ambition is to use the anniversary as a catalyst to strengthen people's relationship with the Runnymede landscape. People have come to this special place for at least 4000 years, and its significance continues to evolve as a place of recreation and memorialisation. The Magna Carta anniversary is therefore an opportunity to celebrate afresh the many layers of this historic landscape, and to work with partners to promote its conservation and presentation for future generations.

The Reeds of Runnymede

by Rudyard Kipling, 1922

At Runnymede, at Runnymede!
    What say the reeds at Runnymede?
The lissom reeds that give and take,
That bend so far, but never break,
They keep the sleepy Thames awake
    With tales of John at Runnymede.

At Runnymede, at Runnymede,
Oh, hear the reeds at Runnymede:–
'You mustn't sell, delay, deny,
A freeman's right or liberty.
It makes the stubborn Englishry –
    We saw 'em roused at Runnymede!

'When through our ranks the Barons came,
With little thought of praise or blame,
But resolute to play the game,
    They lumbered up to Runnymede;
And there they launched in solid line
The first attack on Right Divine –
The curt, uncompromising "Sign!"
    That settled John at Runnymede.

'At Runnymede, at Runnymede,
Your rights were won at Runnymede!
No freeman shall be fined or bound,
    Or dispossessed of freehold ground,
Except by lawful judgment found
And passed upon him by his peers!
Forget not, after all these years,
    The Charter signed at Runnymede.'

And still when Mob or Monarch lays
Too rude a hand on English ways,
The whisper wakes, the shudder plays,
    Across the reeds at Runnymede.
And Thames, that knows the moods of Kings,
And crowds and priests and suchlike things,
Rolls deep and dreadful as he brings
    Their warning down from Runnymede!